# MONEY TROUBLE

The Corner Kids

Written by Larry Dane Brimner • Illustrated by Christine Tripp

Children's Press®
A Division of Scholastic Inc.
New York • Toronto • London • Auckland • Sydney
Mexico City • New Delhi • Hong Kong
Danbury, Connecticut

For Lee Bennett Hopkins
—L.D.B.

For my daughter Elizabeth
—C.T.

Reading Consultants
**Linda Cornwell**
Coordinator of School Quality and Professional Improvement
(Indiana State Teachers Association)

**Katharine A. Kane**
Education Consultant
(Retired, San Diego County Office of Education and San Diego State University)

Library of Congress Cataloging-in-Publication Data

Brimner, Larry Dane.
 Money trouble / by Larry Dane Brimner ; illustrated by Christine Tripp.
  p. cm. — (Rookie choices)
 Summary: Alex learns a lesson about telling the truth when he thinks he has lost
the money his mother gave him to buy milk.
 ISBN 0-516-22155-8 (lib. bdg.)          0-516-25976-8 (pbk.)
 [1. Honesty—Fiction.] I. Tripp, Christine, ill. II. Title. III. Series.
 PZ7.B767 Mo 2001
 [E]—dc21
                                           00-047369

This book is about **responsibility.**

"I'm leaving for the library, Mom,"
Alex said.

"Don't forget to pick up milk on the way home," his mother said. She tucked a five dollar bill into his pocket.

Alex dashed out the door.

Alex met up with his friends Gabby and Three J at the library. They called themselves the Corner Kids.

"Let's find seats," said Three J. "We don't want to miss the show."

"I'll catch up," said Alex. "I want to get a book."

In no time, Alex was back.
"I can't wait to read this!" he said.

"Shhh!" said Gabby.
"The show is starting."

Alex marked his place.

A clown in a fuzzy
orange wig said,
"Introducing . . .
Amazing Matilda!"
A little white dog
sprang out of a box.

After the show, the Corner Kids
stopped at Two Sisters' Market.

Alex put the milk on the counter.
He reached in his pocket.

"The money," he said.
"It's gone!"

"Are you sure?" asked Three J.

"Check your pockets," said Gabby.

"Maybe you dropped it," said Three J.

"Maybe," said Alex.

The Corner Kids looked everywhere.

Later, Alex sighed.
"I guess I better go," he said.

21

Alex tried to sneak in,
but the door squeaked. *Squeak!*

"Hi, Alex!" His mother smiled.
"Did you remember the milk?"

"Yes," Alex said. It wasn't really a lie.
He had *remembered*, but saying
it made his stomach feel bumpy.

"Then where is it?" she asked.
Alex bit his bottom lip.

"Alex?" said his mother.

"Somebody took the money," he said.

"Are you sure?" his mother asked.

Alex thought. He thought some more.
Then he remembered something.

Alex opened his book.
He found the money!

"I thought I lost it," he said.
"I was afraid you would get mad."

"Perhaps," his mother said.
"But we can only solve problems
when we know the truth."
Alex nodded.

"I know a way to solve this problem,"
his mother said.

They walked to Two Sisters' Market together.

TWO SISTERS' MARKET

STOP

31

## ABOUT THE AUTHOR

Larry Dane Brimner studied literature and writing at San Diego State University and taught school for twenty years. The author of more than seventy-five books for children, many of them Children's Press titles, he enjoys meeting young readers and writers when he isn't at his computer.

## ABOUT THE ILLUSTRATOR

Christine Tripp lives in Ottawa, Canada, with her husband Don; four grown children—Elizabeth, Erin, Emily, and Eric; son-in-law Jason; grandsons Brandon and Kobe; four cats; and one very large, scruffy puppy named Jake.